FIND YOUR TALENT

MAKE A MOVIE!

Jim Pipe

ARCTURUS

This edition first published in 2012 by Arcturus Publishing

Distributed by Black Rabbit Books
P. O. Box 3263
Mankato
Minnesota MN 56002

Printed in China

Library of Congress Cataloging-in-Publication Data

Pipe, Jim, 1966-
  Make a movie! / by Jim Pipe.
    p. cm. -- (Find your talent)
  Includes index.
  ISBN 978-1-84858-573-7 (hardcover, library bound : alk. paper)
  1. Motion pictures--Production and direction--Juvenile literature. 2. Motion picture authorship--Juvenile literature. I. Title.
  PN1995.9.P7P526 2013
  791.4302'33--dc23

                          2011051445

The right of Jim Pipe to be identified as the author of this work has been asserted by him in accordance with the Copyright, Designs and Patents Act 1988.

Text: Jim Pipe
Editors: Joe Harris and Sarah Eason
Design: Paul Myerscough
Cover design: Akihiro Nakayama

Picture credits:
Cover images: Shutterstock: Dariush M ct, Phil Date bl, Fer Gregory tc, JHershPhoto ccl, Kosoff tl, Stephen McSweeny cr, Monkey Business Images br, NemesisINC bc, Michele Perbellini ccr, Triff tr, Andrey Valerevich Kiselev cl.
Interior images: Library of Congress: 7l; Shutterstock: AleksKey 25tr, Bertrand Benoit 6cl, Blankartist 4bl, Gualtiero Boffi 19br, Sean De Burca 13tr, Sascha Burkard 10–11, Cinemafestival 7cr, 23br, Creatista 18–19tc, Cybrain 24tr, Dariush M 01, Deklofenak 26bl, Dario Diament 21t, Helga Esteb 15br, Marcello Farina 9bl, Alexey Fursov 14bl, Haider 23cl, Korionov 9cr, Kuzma 20bl, Sergey Lavrentev 4–5tc, 17cr, Left Eyed Photography 5br, Olly 9tr, Pavel Losevsky 3bl, 22bl, Mateo Pearson 14–15tc, Michele Perbellini 20cr, Lev Radin 29t, Aspen Rock 28cr, Sam72 24bl, Stanalex 26–27tc, StudioSmart 18br, Andrey Valerevich Kiselev 3cl, 16r, Wavebreakmedia ltd 12bl, Lisa F. Young 17bl, Zurijeta 8cr.

SL002139US
Supplier 03 Date 0412 Print run 1449

CONTENTS

FIND YOUR TALENT!

Many of the best writers and directors started out with short films, or "shorts." Most film festivals include shorts, giving new filmmakers a chance to show what they can do. Would you like to see your film in a theater or at the Oscars? If so, making a short film is easier than you think!

Making a film takes teamwork. This crew is setting up the lighting.

GO FOR IT: TEAM PICKS

Here are some of the key roles and skills in a film crew:

- The writer creates an interesting story, good dialogue, and believable characters.
- The director will explain his or her vision for the film to the cast and crew.
- The producer works out the budget and makes sure everything happens on time.
- The camera and sound crew operate the equipment.
- The makeup, costume, and design team ensure the actors and set look good.
- The actors bring the script to life.
- The editor helps the director to choose the best takes from the shoot and put them all together.

EARLY DAYS: Do It Yourself

British director Shane Meadows started off by making over 30 shorts. In one of his first films, *Where's the Money, Ronnie?*, Shane played all the parts. He also operated the camera and edited the film. Making a film on your own can be done, but it is hard work!

You don't need to build a spectacular set to make a movie. Learn how to find a good location (on page 14).

The dream team Making movies is a team effort—very few people make films as a one-person crew with no actors. So, if you are planning to make a short film, it is easiest to work in a team. Do not try to do everything yourself—ask around. You will be surprised how many people will work on your film for free.

Let's go! In this book, you'll find out that making your own short film can be a lot of fun. You will also discover some of the real-life stories behind a few of the world's most popular films, and find out how filmmakers have turned their hobby into a fantastic career.

Actor Robert Pattison has starred in the blockbuster *Twilight* and in short films such as *The Summer House*.

WHAT SORT OF FILM?

Short films can be about anything—the only limit (other than budget) is your imagination. Start off by bouncing ideas around with your friends, but be realistic. Mind-blowing ideas are no good if you cannot afford to shoot them!

What type of film?

There are many different types, or "genres" of film. Musicals, science fiction movies, and action films often need a big budget. However, many horror movies have been made on a small budget. Comedy is another good option— cheap sets and costumes are easy to find and can add to the humor.

Be realistic when planning your film—it takes a large budget to produce a sci-fi movie with lots of special effects.

GO FOR IT: THE PLAN

There are four main stages to making a film:
- Develop your idea by coming up with the main theme or plot, then write the script.
- Get organized—cast the actors and rehearse the script. There are also lots of other jobs such as finding props or a location. Share these out among the team.
- Carry out the shoot—this is the all-important time when the film is shot.
- Finally, put it all together! At this stage, it is best if just the editor, director, and producer edit the film. If too many people get involved, you can lose the focus of the film.

The budget Before you start filming, work out how much money you can spend on the project and what you want to spend it on. It's no good starting a project if you can't finish it!

EARLY DAYS: No actors required

Why not practice your filmmaking skills by copying a famous movie scene using puppets or toys? This is how Francis Ford Coppola, one of the most famous directors, started out. He shot short films using a homemade puppet theater after an illness forced him to stay at home.

Inspirational director Francis Ford Coppola started out with puppets—and ended up making Oscar-winning movies.

Short and sweet The shorter your film, the less it will cost to make! You can tell a great story in as little as 30 seconds. You don't even need talking parts—watch a Charlie Chaplin film to see the magic of a silent short film.

Charlie Chaplin could create a very funny scene with just a few simple props.

CREATE A SCRIPT

Film projects start with just a good idea. Ideas are not easy to come up with, so it helps to start by watching other short films. These will show you what can be done.

Come late, leave early Writing a script can be tough—you need to tell your story and develop characters in a short space of time. However, you can achieve a great deal with just two or three main characters. Avoid spending too much time explaining what is going on. Instead, start the film where your story really kicks off and end it as soon as your story is told.

GO FOR IT: WRITER TIPS

- Start your script with a strong idea. Remember, one page of a script is one minute on screen!
- Create characters that people will remember.
- Listen to how people talk in real life and apply to your script. You can get great story ideas from unusual TV or newspaper reports.
- Rewrite, rewrite, rewrite! Take a few days off, then come back to your script. Read it out aloud.
- Test your script out on friends and relatives. Listen to their feedback.

It takes discipline to write a script. Set aside time to work on it, and don't get distracted!

Show, don't tell A film is about telling stories in pictures, so when you write the script, try to "set the scene." When your character moves to the window, does he stumble, dash, or saunter? Putting these details in the script will focus the story. It's also much easier to edit your ideas on paper before you start shooting.

Whether you are making a horror film or a love story, always start with a dramatic scene or shot that will grab the viewer's attention.

For legendary director Quentin Tarantino, moviemaking is all about telling a great story.

INSIDE STORY: MOVIE MOODS

What mood do you want for the film? The choice of music can make a big difference. American director Quentin Tarantino once said: "To me, movies and music go hand in hand. When I'm writing a script, one of the first things I do is find the music I'm going to play for the opening sequence."

MAKE A SHOT LIST

You can shoot a whole scene from one angle. Or you can add drama by shooting the same scene from different angles, or from close-up and far away. After filming, these shots can be edited together.

These three shots show how shooting one scene from three different points of view can help to tell the story.

WIDE SHOT

All in the planning A shot list describes what you will be shooting, including the music, props, and effects in each shot. With a detailed shot list, if you have to cut something out during a shoot, you will know which scene to move on to next.

Different shots Learn the terms for each shot. A wide shot captures the whole scene. A medium shot shows the actors from the waist up. A close-up focuses on a key feature—for example, a face or an important object. Cutaways are shots of things away from the main action. In panning shots, the camera sweeps across the scene.

MEDIUM SHOT

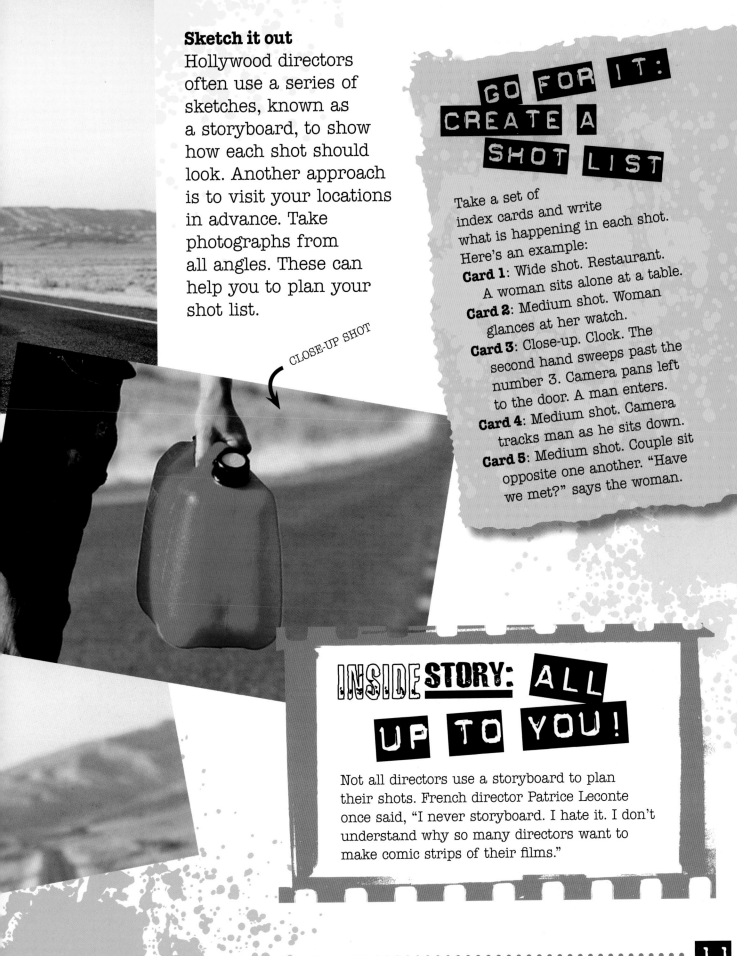

Sketch it out

Hollywood directors often use a series of sketches, known as a storyboard, to show how each shot should look. Another approach is to visit your locations in advance. Take photographs from all angles. These can help you to plan your shot list.

CLOSE-UP SHOT

Take a set of index cards and write what is happening in each shot. Here's an example:

Card 1: Wide shot. Restaurant. A woman sits alone at a table.

Card 2: Medium shot. Woman glances at her watch.

Card 3: Close-up. Clock. The second hand sweeps past the number 3. Camera pans left to the door. A man enters.

Card 4: Medium shot. Camera tracks man as he sits down.

Card 5: Medium shot. Couple sit opposite one another. "Have we met?" says the woman.

INSIDE STORY: ALL UP TO YOU!

Not all directors use a storyboard to plan their shots. French director Patrice Leconte once said, "I never storyboard. I hate it. I don't understand why so many directors want to make comic strips of their films."

CASTING ACTORS

With any type of film, you need a great cast. A good actor can make your film come alive. Do you know any good actors among your friends or at your school? If not, your drama teacher may be able to help.

Who's who? The first step is to create a list of the actors you need. Think about what you have in mind for each character. What age and build are you looking for? Do you need a particular look or haircut?

GO FOR IT: FIND YOUR STARS!

Auditions can sound scary, but they can be a chance to have some fun:

- Read through a couple of scenes in character.
- Ask the actors to improvise a scene for a couple of minutes.
- Try "hot seating." Ask an actor to answer all sorts of questions while staying in their character.
- When the auditions are over, make your decisions about who to cast in your film.
- Try not to feel too guilty about rejecting anyone—but be polite!

Choosing the stars Actors should look relaxed and natural when they are playing other people. They need to be able to say their lines clearly. It can make things easier if you find good actors who already look and sound like the characters they are playing.

Work together to decide exactly how you see each character before the casting begins.

CASTING

Everyone feels a little nervous during an audition. It's all part of being an actor!

Working with actors The director's job is to help the actors work well together. Try to get them excited about their roles. Rehearse several times so that they have a chance to develop their parts and get a feel for the other actors. You won't have time to do things over and over during the shoot.

EARLY DAYS: Love at first film

The romantic Irish film *Once* shows what can be done with a small budget and unknown actors. The two stars, Glen Hansard and Markéta Irglová, were musicians. They did not have much acting experience. But it helped that they fell in love while making the movie!

LOCATION, LOCATION!

A big question for every director and producer is: where will the film be shot? You probably won't have the money to work in a film studio or build a set. The secret is to find one or two free locations that suit the mood of the film.

Go local Scout around your town for interesting places where you can do the shoot. Check out parks, woods, or beaches for outdoor scenes. You can shoot indoor scenes in a cast member's house. If you want to shoot in a school or local business, ask for permission to use their buildings over the weekend.

An empty warehouse is great for an action movie. A romantic comedy? Maybe not.

GO FOR IT: FINDING A LOCATION

Use these tips to source a good location:
- The location should match the script. If a scene is set in a castle, it would feel wrong if it was filmed in a modern house.
- If you cannot get the location you want, be flexible. Another great location may be worth changing the script for.
- Make sure you have room to move the camera around. There also needs to be space for the crew to get out of the way when shooting.
- If you want a cramped feel, make a larger space look small rather than filming in a closet!

Space it out Check out how much space there is in each location. Then work out how your actors are going to move during the scenes. Do they need to walk into or out of a shot, or move close to the camera? This "walk though" needs to be rehearsed in advance. Watch carefully for movements that look odd.

Film director Danny Boyle has used low-budget locations as well as expensive settings for his films.

Before you pick an exotic location to shoot your film, have a good look at your budget! Can you afford it?

INSIDE STORY: TRAPPED

Some films use very few locations. In the film *127 Hours*, many scenes were shot in a narrow canyon where a hiker had been trapped. Cramped locations like this can make the audience feel trapped, too. The film's director, Danny Boyle, described it as "an action movie with a guy who can't move."

THE RIGHT LOOK

Every director wants to make his or her film look as great as possible. That means finding the right costumes and props, and using makeup on the actors. It is easiest if your film is set in the present—you'll find that the props and clothes you need are all around you!

Historical costumes look amazing. But make sure you get the hairstyle and accessories right, too.

Look the part Every character needs to have clothes and jewelry that are suited for his or her part. Look for clothes that fit the personality of the characters or add to the mood of the film. If you need something very specific, such as a historical costume, you can go to a costume store. If you ask nicely, you might even get them to do a deal!

Renting a costume is usually cheaper than trying to make it yourself.

Set it up You may not be able to build a set, but props can help to create the right mood. During shooting, set dressers arrange objects on the film set. They move furniture to the right position, hang pictures, and put out decorative items, such as vases. The set should not look too neat. Real homes rarely look like show homes or tidy hotel rooms.

GO FOR IT: MAKEUP

Ask someone experienced at using makeup to help out:

- Apply powder to stop faces looking shiny on camera.
- Use a yellow theatrical color neutralizer to get rid of purple under-eye shadows. Light green gets rid of red around the nose.
- To make an actor look injured, make some fake blood by mixing corn syrup, red food coloring and a touch of blue food coloring.

Want more gore? Special makeup kits can create very realistic cuts and injuries. No pain, all gain!

INSIDE STORY: CLOTHES SPEAK

Oscar-winning costume designer Colleen Atwood once said, "Costumes are the first impression that you have of the character before they open their mouth—it really does establish who they are."

AND ACTION!

If you don't own your own camera, you may be able to borrow one from a relative or from your school. First, learn how to take a simple shot well. Then you can start to experiment with different methods of filming.

Know your camera You can make a film with lots of different devices, from a camcorder to a smart phone. Whatever you use, spend as much time as you can experimenting with it. Learn how to focus on your subject. See how different angles change the mood of a shot. Watch videos and films and work out how a particular shot was taken.

Keep it steady A tripod will help you to achieve a steady, smooth shot. You can also steady yourself by leaning on a wall or piece of furniture.

Practice shooting with a tripod. Use one hand on the focus and the other to pan and tilt.

EARLY DAYS: Cart style

Mexican director Robert Rodriguez used a shopping cart and a wheelchair to move his camera about when he made his first film. He once said, "Don't be told something is impossible. There's always a way."

To get the best out of your camera:

- Frame your shot by keeping the camera steady and in focus.
- Use one eye to look through the viewfinder, and the other to watch your surroundings.
- When you are happy with the frame, press "record"—remember to make sure that you are actually recording!
- Learn to walk backward as you film—ask someone to place their hand in the middle of your back to guide you.
- Don't get too close to your cast—actors feel more comfortable if you give them some room.
- Avoid zooming and panning as you film. It's best to keep the camera steady.

Ensure that your close-up shot does not cut off the actor's head or distort their face in an unattractive way!

Frame it! Framing a shot means choosing what to include or leave out. Try not to chop off the tops of the actors' heads. Watch the edge of the frame to make sure the actors' faces are not cut in half. Try different angles—you can kneel down to shoot a crawling baby or stand on a chair to shoot actors from above.

A Point of View (POV) shot is taken from the viewpoint of a character in the film—such as a killer!

SOUND AND LIGHTING

Films need to look great, but they should sound good, too. If the voices are muffled or you can hear the wind blowing in the background, it can really spoil your film.

Recording sound Record the dialogue as well as you can during the shoot. You can ask the actors to record their parts later on, but it is really hard to match the video. If you are using the microphone on your camera, try to find a balance between getting the shot you want and picking up the actors' voices.

INSIDE STORY: SOUND ADVICE

George Lucas, director of the *Star Wars* movies, realised the importance of sound in his films and once said: "The sound and music are 50 percent of the entertainment in a movie."

Booms are usually held high so they don't appear in the shot.

Using a camera microphone? Keep close to the actors to pick up their dialogue clearly.

If you have lights on set, be careful. They can get very hot.

Microphones If you can, borrow another microphone. Put this as close to the actors as possible but keep it out of the shot! Sounds such as a background noise can be added using audio clips later.

Keep it natural Natural light can work well, so try shooting underneath a roof light or near windows. If the room is a little dark, you can make the scenes brighter using software when you edit the film. However, most camcorders do not work very well in dim lighting. If there are night scenes in your script, think about rewriting it.

GO FOR IT: RECORDING TRICKS

To get the best recording:
- Use a boom (or a broom handle) to hold a microphone close to the actors, usually over their heads.
- If you are using a microphone, you will need a laptop to record the sound.
- Record a "wild track." This is a minute or two of quiet in the room where you are filming. You can use this to cover up unwelcome background noises (such as traffic sounds) during editing.
- If you are recording outside, put a sock over the microphone to cut out the noise from the wind.

THE SHOOT

You have your cast, crew, equipment, locations, script, and props in place. Now for the really exciting part—the shoot! Make sure you are well prepared and everyone in your team knows what the plan is.

Quick work You can shoot the same scene several times over to get different camera angles. But there is a quicker way. Let's say an actor has a long speech you want to shoot from two angles. Shoot the first half with a medium shot, then zoom into a close-up shot. When you edit the film, replace the zooming-in section with a cutaway shot (see page 10).

EARLY DAYS:
Lights, camera, fight!

Many new directors are surprised at how long a shoot can take. No matter how long your day is, try to enjoy it. Whatever happens, remember that screaming and shouting will not get good results!

This camera operator must zoom in on the actors to keep the crew out of the frame.

The perfect shoot Before shooting a scene, read the script. Then walk through the action before your first "camera rehearsal." Once you're sure all the equipment is working, run through the scene with the actors. If you are lucky, everything should happen as planned on the first take. If you are unsure, do a couple more takes.

Rehearsals help a camera operator to learn the actors' movements.

GO FOR IT: TAKE NOTES!

Create a sheet of notes or an email with all the information for each day of a shoot. This "call sheet" should include:

- contact numbers of the cast and crew
- a list of scenes to shoot each day and who is in each shot
- who is responsible for first aid on set
- photocopies of maps or directions that show how to get to and from the shoot

INSIDE STORY:
PLAN B?

Do not worry if things don't turn out exactly as you planned. It might make your film better! As American director Spike Lee said, "A lot of times you get credit for stuff in your movies you did not intend to be there."

Director Spike Lee uses moving cameras, extreme angles, and tight close-ups to give scenes tension.

ALL IN THE EDIT

A film really comes together when you edit it. This means arranging, adding, or cutting video clips to make a complete film. It's easy to do on a computer using software such as iMovie or Premiere. You could ask a teacher whether you can use video editing software at school. You can learn how to use it by watching tutorials on the Internet.

The word "cutting" comes from a time when editors actually cut up film reels when editing a film.

Capture it! It is easy to transfer or "capture" video footage from a camcorder. Most cameras come with a cable that you just plug into your computer. Try to use the fastest computer you can. You also need lots of storage space as video files are huge. Three minutes of footage takes up about one gigabyte of memory.

Most camcorders are very easy to hook up to a computer.

GO FOR IT: PUT IT ALL TOGETHER

A finished film needs:
- a title at the beginning
- a set of "shots" cut together to tell a story
- variety—change the camera angle every few seconds
- a good soundtrack
- credits at the end

You can download free video and sound editing programs from the Internet.

The edit Once you have all the unedited or "raw" footage on your computer, the fun really begins. First, select the shots you are going to use. Then use the software to seamlessly join the shots together. Make sure sound recorded at the shoot is in time with the video. Think about what else you can add, such as music. Always make sure that you use music recorded by friends or that is copyright free (free to use without payment) if you are going to enter your film in a competition.

INSIDE STORY: THE FINAL FIX

The editing stage is your chance to fix things that were not quite right on the shoot. Here is some advice from the great Indian director Satyajit Ray: "Particularly in the final stages I always find that I'm rushed. It's dangerous when you're rushed in the editing stage."

FIND AN AUDIENCE

Once you've finished your video, organize a cast and crew screening. It's a good excuse for a party and you can get useful feedback. But how do you get other people to watch your short?

Get online You can upload your video onto a web site such as YouTube. However, general sites like this often claim the rights to anything that is uploaded to their pages. It might be better to upload your film to web sites that want to help new talent, such as the Shortie Awards.

You don't have to show your film at a theater to find an audience. Just post it online and spread the word.

You could persuade your actors to promote your film in full costume!

Create a web site A web site is a great way to promote your film. It is also a good place to let people know who you are and allows you to provide background information about the film. Show photos of the cast and crew in action. You could email a link to your web site to people who are film reviewers and bloggers, and ask them for feedback. You can also set up profile pages on social network sites.

Got the bug? If you enjoyed making your film, why not start work on your next one? You can tell people about it while promoting your first film. You never know who might want to help you out the next time.

STEP UP A GEAR

Once you have made a few short films, you might want to get more serious. Here are some ideas for taking the next step toward shooting your first blockbuster movie!

Martin Scorsese is just one of many famous directors who started out making short films.

Soundtrack Get a local band to create the soundtrack to your next film. You can listen to their tracks and decide whether any of them suit a particular scene. Or they might be willing to write some new material for your film. Send them a copy of the finished video so they know how long each scene is.

Special effects These days, great effects can be achieved with editing software. Every new trick you can learn will add something to the next film you make. In 2011, the alien invasion film *Monsters* was filmed using just two main actors! All the effects were then created on director Gareth Edwards's home computer.

The right stuff If you want to submit your film to festivals and web sites, you need to make sure you own the rights. Rights is another way of saying who owns the film. You also need to get permission from all the actors who appear in your film – even if they say nothing in the movie!

Submit your short to a film festival and you could find yourself on the red carpet.

Find an agent If you've made a popular and successful short film, it could be worth sending a copy to an agent (check out the Film Network web site for guidance about how to find an agent—see page 31). An agent will have lots of contacts in the film industry and might be able to recommend you for a project.

Big budget? If someone is willing to put some money into your next film, you will need to work out how best to spend it. That means a real budget. Think about things like transport, makeup, costumes, props, equipment hire and the cost of producing a DVD.

Spread the word You stand a better chance of success if people are writing or talking about your films. Keep sending links of your latest films to reviewers at local newspapers or film bloggers.

GLOSSARY

audio clip a short sound file

audition a trial or test performance where an actor or singer shows off their skills

boom a long pole

budget a list or estimate of costs

camcorder a video camera and recorder combined into one

canyon a deep, narrow valley with very steep sides

cast the actors in a play or film

character a person in a story or play

corn syrup a sticky, runny food sweetener

costume store a store where you can rent costumes

cramped a very small space

credits a list of the cast and crew on a film

crew the team who make a film

device a machine or gadget

dialogue the speaking parts in a play or film

director the person in charge of the creative side of a film

download to extract a file from the Internet

edit to cut, arrange, or correct a film or book

editor the person in charge of editing a film or book

effects tricks to make something look different on screen

establish to set up

flexible easy to change or bend

focus to concentrate on something

footage an amount of film or video

gigabyte 1,000 megabytes, an amount of storage space on a computer

improvise to make up on the spot

location the place where you shoot a film

mood atmosphere

muffled a dull sound

musicals films where the actors sing

operate to use or handle

Oscar a famous film-industry award

permission to be allowed to do something

plot the storyline

producer the person in charge of a film

profile pages web site pages featuring information about you or your film

promote to tell people about an event or product

props objects used on a film set

rehearse to practice

reject to turn someone down

reviewer people who assess music for a living

rights the ownership of a book or film

role a character or part played by an actor

scene a setting for part of a play or film

screening a showing of a film

script the text of a film

sequence how one thing follows after another

set the scenery and props

set dressers the people who arrange the set

shot list a list of all the shots in a film

software a computer program

soundtrack the music in a film

specific something special or unique

surroundings the area around a thing or place

theatrical color neutralizer makeup that helps an actor's skin look smoother and more natural on camera

theme the main idea in a film

tracks sound recordings

tripod a support for a camera, with three legs

viewfinder the device you look through on a camera

zoom to adjust the lens of a camera to appear closer or farther away from an object

FURTHER INFORMATION

Books

Filmmaking for Teens: Pulling Off Your Shorts by Troy Lanier and Clay Nichols (Michael Wiese, 2010)

Kids Guide to Moviemaking by Shelley Frost (CreateSpace, 2011)

Movie Maker: The Ultimate Guide to Making Films by Tim Grabham, Suridh Hassan, Dave Reeve, and Clare Richards (Candlewick, 2010)

Screenwriting for Dummies by John Logan and Laura Schellhardt (John Wiley & Sons, 2008)

Stand-Out Shorts: Shooting and Sharing Your Films Online by Russell Evans (Focal Press, 2010)

Web sites

Rotten Tomatoes
One of the best ways to learn about filmmaking is to watch great movies. This site has reviews of thousands of films to help you pick the very best!:
www.rottentomatoes.com

The Shortie Awards
These awards focus on "nurturing imagination and celebrating stories from all over the world," aimed at filmmakers age 7 to 18:
www.shortieawards.org

Short Films
A social network that allows filmmakers to upload their short films and create their own blog:
www.shortfilms.com

Simply Scripts
Links to hundreds of free, downloadable movie scripts and screenplays:
www.simplyscripts.com

The Smalls
A showcase for short films and music, helping filmmakers and musicians to get work. You can watch lots of great short films here:
www.thesmalls.com

Trigger Street Labs
A site where aspiring screenwriters and directors can get their work seen and reviewed:
www.labs.triggerstreet.com

Apps

iFilmmaker Pro Lite
A mobile guide to hundreds of tips and tricks used by filmmakers, with sections on editing, directing, writing a script, and acting.

iMovie
A fun video editing app for the iPhone. You can even create a video postcard of your day at the beach and publish it on the web!

INDEX